BIKING
IN
VIKINGLAND

Where to Go
What to Expect
How to Get There

by
MARLYS MICKELSON

Revised 1993
ADVENTURE PUBLICATIONS, INC.
P.O. Box 269
Cambridge, Minnesota 55008

© copyright 1993

ISBN 0-934860-00-9

Also by Marlys Mickelson
SEAT YOURSELF
A Complete Guide to Twin Cities Arenas,
Auditoriums and Theatres

First printing 1988
Second printing 1990
Third printing 1991

Front cover photo: West Duluth to Carlton segment
of the Willard Munger Trail. Photo by
Paul Sundberg, Two Harbors, MN

Back cover photo: DNR photo, Dan Ruda

This book is dedicated to a diverse group of energetic individuals whose mutual interest in physical activity, ecology, conservation and the great outdoors evolved into an ever-widening circle of friends who call themselves the *Weakenders*. ™

ACKNOWLEDGEMENTS

My sincere appreciation for the cooperation and assistance given by the Departments of Transportation, and Natural Resources and the Office of Tourism of the State of Minnesota. Also the Division of Tourism and the Department of Natural Resources Bureau of Parks and Recreation of the State of Wisconsin.

And especially to my husband Phil for his support and assistance.

INTRODUCTION

If you like bicycling and everything that goes with it — good exercise, friendship and being outdoors — you'll love this book.

This easy-to-use guide highlights improved, off-highway routes specifically designated for biking and hiking, but also includes information on thousands of miles of mountain bike trails in Minnesota and Wisconsin.

Whatever your age or biking skill, this guide is for individuals, groups or families who want to bike at their leisure on trails that don't mean spending an entire day on a bicycle seat.

In the trail section, we've put together comprehensive trail maps, trail length and other pertinent trailhead information. Attractions in surrounding communities are listed, too.

Biking in Vikingland tells you where to go, what to expect and how to get there.

In Celebration of Cycling

TO WHEEL quietly up and down hill and across the valley, miles away from so-called civilization, and yet knowing that with a good bicycle miles mean but little; to wheel along drinking in the perfumes of the morning with the song of the birds, and at even, thankful for the matchless glow in the west and the music of cow-bells; to wheel silently at sunset into some peaceful village where your guidebook bids you expect a welcome — all this is worth celebrating.

— *Philip C. Hubert, Jr.,*
Scribner's Magazine, *1895*

CONTENTS

Page

An Overview 1
  Minnesota Department of Transportation Bikeways 2
  Addresses, Phone Numbers, Accommodations 5
  Wisconsin Addresses, Phone Numbers 8

Rail Trails 11
  Cannon Valley Trail 12
  Douglas State Trail 16
  Heartland State Trail 20
  Luce Line State Trail 24
  Willard Munger State Trail 28
    Carlton – West Duluth Segment 28
    Gateway Segment 32
    Hinckley Fire Trail Segment 36
  Root River State Trail 40
  Sakatah Singing Hills State Trail 44

State Park Trails 50
Regional Parks 54
  Bunker Hills Regional Park 55
Hennepin Parks
  Baker Park Reserve 56
  Carver Park Reserve 57
  Cleary Lake Regional Park 58
  Elm Creek Park Reserve 59
  Hyland Lake Park Reserve 60
  Lake Rebecca Park Reserve 61
  North Hennepin Trail Corridor 62
Minneapolis Parks and Recreation
  Grand Rounds Parkway System 63
St. Paul Parks and Recreation
  Como Park 64
  Crosby Farm/Hidden Falls 64
  Phalen 65

Western Wisconsin 67
  Red Cedar State Park Trail 68
  Chippewa River State Park Trail 71
  Great River State Park Trail 72
  LaCrosse River State Park Trail 76
  Elroy-Sparta State Park Trail 78
  "400" State Trail 82

Mountain Biking 85

Safety and Equipment 99

AN OVERVIEW

Minnesota Department
of Transportation
Bikeways

Addresses
Phone Numbers
Accommodations

Wisconsin Addresses
Phone Numbers

Biking in Vikingland can happen in many different ways, in many different places, requiring all degrees of skill and endurance. Although the emphasis of this book is primarily off-road bike trails, the biking enthusiast should be aware of the many alternatives offered by Minnesota and Wisconsin.

For the most comprehensive and detailed information and maps on biking in Minnesota and Wisconsin, we can refer you to no better source than the *Explore Minnesota Bikeways* maps published by the Minnesota Department of Transportation and the *Bicycle Escape Guide* published by the Wisconsin Division of Tourism.

Minnesota Bikeways maps divide the state into four sections and the Twin Cities metro area into two sections. At the present time five of the six are available. You may order the northeast, northwest, southeast, metro east and metro west by mail. The southwest section is being developed and will be available in 1993. **For information on the southwest quadrant, telephone the Department of Transportation maps section at 612-296-2216.**

In addition to the DNR-maintained rail trails which are detailed in this book, you will find accurate maps of trails and bike paths in towns and along highways which are suited for biking and of particular interest to long distance riders. Roads are color coded to identify bicycling suitability for your plans. Your investment in each of these maps would be well worth the cost. In addition to mail order, the Dept. of Transportation maps are available in many bike stores and some map stores.

In addition to the metro east and metro west maps, the four state section maps include insets of outstate cities with bikeways. Off-street bike paths in northeast Minnesota are indicated in the inset maps of Duluth, Grand Rapids, Hibbing and Virginia. In the southeast, inset maps showing off-street biking are Faribault, Mankato, Owatonna, Red Wing, Rochester, St. Cloud and Winona. The map of the northwest quadrant will detail routes in Detroit Lakes, Grand Forks/E. Grand Forks, Fergus Falls and Fargo/Moorhead, while the southwest map includes inset maps of Fairmont and Marshall.

East
Grand
Forks

International
Falls

Bemidji

Northeast

Northwest

Grand ● ● Hibbing
Rapids

● Moorhead

Duluth ●

**Minneapolis-St. Paul
Metro Area**

● Brainerd

Little Falls ●

Metro
West

Metro
East

*Southwest
map
available
in 1994*

● St. Cloud

Twin
Cities

Southeast

● Mankato ● Rochester

Winona ●

Downtown Minneapolis
appears on both the
Metro East and the
Metro West maps.

● Albert Lea

Each map contains information regarding:

- Road analysis for bicycle usage
- Location of paved road shoulders
- Location of off-road bikeways
- Location of bike-pedestrian bridges
- Controlled access roads (bicycles prohibited)
- Historical and cultural attractions
- Public parklands and facilities

Map Price Schedule

MAP	QUANTITY	
	1-19	20 or more
Southeast (SE)	$3.00 ea.	$2.40 ea.
Northeast (NE)	$3.00 ea.	$2.40 ea.
Metro East	$2.00 ea.	$1.60 ea.
Metro West	$2.00 ea.	$1.60 ea.
Postage per *order*	$2.00	$2.00

Prices subject to change without notice.

6.5% sales tax must be added to each order
for MN residents only.

Mail Map Orders To:

Minnesota Department of Transportation
John Ireland Boulevard
Room B-20
St. Paul MN 55155
(no phone order accepted)

or

Minnesota Bookstore
117 University Avenue (Ford Bldg.)
St. Paul MN 55155
612-297-3000 or 1 (800) 657-3757
Phone Orders Accepted
MasterCard, VISA, Discover,
American Express

Minnesota is biking country. It is the leader in the development of bicycle trails with 570 miles of bike paths available to approximately 2.8 million riders. Minnesota is one of 24 states with a full-time bike coordinator. For additional information, safety brochures, etc., contact:

> State Bicycle Coordinator
> State Bicycle Advisory Board
> 807 Transportation Building
> St. Paul MN 55155
> 612-297-1838

The Minnesota Department of Natural Resources has converted 250 miles of railroad right-of-way that offer a quiet biking experience through scenic areas on a level, less than three percent grade. Parking space is provided and rest areas generally include a picnic area, drinking water and restrooms. Individual maps of the nine bicycle trails, state parks with bicycle paths and mountain bike opportunities are available at no charge. Contact:

> Minnesota Department of Natural Resources
> Outdoor Information Center
> Box 40, 500 Lafayette Road
> St. Paul MN 55146
> 612-296-6699
> Within Minnesota, Toll Free: 800-766-6000

In addition to the rail trails the DNR has selected seven weekend tour routes following low use roads. **Southeast Blufflands**: 160 miles; **Southern Farmbelt**: 98 miles; **Minnesota River Valley**: 86 mile linear route, plus a 35 mile loop and a 40 mile loop. In the **Twin Cities Area**: There are two loops, 30 and 33 miles. **Central Hills and Lakes** has three loops of 97, 64, and 30 miles. There is also **Northern Pine and Lakes**: 126 miles; and the **North Shore Highlands**: 50 miles. Trail Explorer Trip Guides are available from the DNR Information Center, address above.

5

The DNR Rail Trails are suitable for wheelchairs and families with young children. Many trails are ideal for family nature studies. Shop carefully for the child carrier that you attach to your bicycle and be certain the youngster is wearing a helmet. Remember to stock water and energy boosters, and that small wheels require many more revolutions than your 27" bicycle.

The Minnesota Office of Tourism has developed free directories for accommodations that you may order by phone or mail. *Explore Minnesota Hotels, Explore Minnesota Motels, Explore Minnesota Resorts, Explore Minnesota Campgrounds* and *Explore Minnesota Bed and Breakfast and Historic Inns,* all available from:

> Minnesota Office of Tourism
> 100 Metro Square
> 121 Seventh Place East
> St. Paul MN 55101
> 800-657-3700
> Metro area: 296-5029

Minnesota has a continuing Rail to Trail acquisition and development program which will improve existing trail systems and take advantage of some of the hundreds of miles of abandoned rail bed remaining in the state. Present plans include the following which will be incorporated in future editions of this book as they are added to the trail system.

> Paul Bunyan:
> Bemidji to Brainerd, about 100 miles which will connect to the Heartland Trail.

> Glacial Lakes:
> Willmar to Richmond – running through Spicer, New London and Hawick, about 34 miles.

Root River Trail extension:
South from Fountain to Harmony. East
from Rushford to Houston and eventually
LaCrescent – estimated 50 miles.

Willar Munger completion:
Connect all the way from Duluth to St. Paul.

Gandy Dancer:
A 90 mile trail originating and ending in
Wisconsin, the Minnesota segment enters at
Danbury and parallels the state line to exit just
south of Superior.

For trail status information, check with
Parks Dept. of Polk County, Balsam Lake;
Burnett County, Grantsburg, or Douglas County,
Superior, all in Wisconsin.

Bike Shorts

• Footwear is important in biking. Choose shoes with a
fairly rigid sole.

• Allow for less efficient braking in wet weather or after
riding through a puddle. Water on your rims and brakes
can double the distance required to stop.

The Wisconsin DNR Bureau of Parks and Recreation has a continuing program of expansion and improvement of its off-road biking systems. Wisconsin currently maintains 320 miles of improved rail-bed trails and lists nearly 5000 miles of off-road trails open to mountain biking. Future additions to their Rails to Trails system include: the Gandy Dancer, from St. Croix Falls to Superior. This trail will enter Minnesota at Danbury, paralleling the Minnesota/Wisconsin border until just south of Superior. The Wiowash is open for 20 miles from Oshkosh to Hortonville an additional 60 miles is in the planning stage.

Most of the 12 rail-bed trails are surfaced with crushed limestone and intersect with numerous small communities providing frequent access, rest and refreshment stops. A daily fee is charged and tags are available from bike shops, designated businesses and /or DNR representatives along the trail. An annual pass is also available. The Wisconsin trails are open from 6:00 A.M. to 11:00 P.M.

For a copy of *Biking Wisconsin's State Park Trails*, send $3.00 plus .15 tax and $1.00 for postage/handling to:

> Wisconsin DNR Bureau of
> Parks and Recreation
> P.O. Box 7921
> Madison WI 53703-7921
> 608-266-2181

The free Wisconsin State Parks Visitor's Guide is also available at that address.

The State of Wisconsin publishes two maps exclusively devoted to biking, one for each half of the state. Either or both are available at no charge. For the *Western Wisconsin Bicycle Escape Guide* and/or *Eastern Wisconsin Bicycle Escape Guide* contact:

Wisconsin Division of Tourism
123 West Washington Avenue
P.O. Box 7606
Madison WI 53707
800-372-2737

MINNESOTA RAIL TRAILS

Cannon Valley Trail

Douglas State Trail

Heartland State Trail

Luce Line State Trail

Willard Munger State Trail
Carlton to W. Duluth Segment
Gateway Segment
Hinckley Fire Segment

Root River State Trail

Sakatah Singing Hills State Trail

Trail length: 19.7 miles

Surface: Blacktop, user fee required

Trailhead east: Old W. Main St. and Bench St. one block off Hwy. 61 in west Red Wing. Parking lot nearby. To downtown Red Wing, you may follow Old West Main along the marked historic route near the Mississippi River.

Mid access: Hwy 19 east from Cannon Falls to Co. Rd 7, north to Welch. Or Hwy 61 east of Miesville to Co. Rd 7 south. Parking, shelter, picnic tables, restrooms and water.

In the area: Visit the beautifully restored St. James Hotel. Consider a Mississippi River cruise on the Princess Red Wing (May – October). For more information on attractions in the area, write to:

> Red Wing Area Chamber of Commerce
> 420 Levee St.
> Red Wing MN 55066
> 612-388-4719

Trailhead west: Although the trail actually starts near 3rd Street in Cannon Falls, parking is limited. Ample parking is available across from the ballpark on E. Stoughton St. Trail access is provided from the east end of the lot.

In the area: Canoeing and tubing on the Cannon River. For more information, write or call:

> Cannon Falls Area Chamber of Commerce
> 103 – 4th St. North
> Cannon Falls MN 55009
> 507-263-2289

For a trail with great scenery in all seasons, shelter from the wind and shade from the hot sun, this is the place to be. The trail follows the Cannon River Valley from Cannon Falls to Red Wing. At 19.7 miles, it is a short one-way ride or a quite manageable two-way trip. Although not a part of the DNR State Trail system, this is a scenic, well-maintained paved trail.

For this gem, we are indebted to a group of private citizens from Cannon Falls, Welch and Red Wing who saw the recreational value of the area. They secured the property and obtained the grants and assistance to improve it and replace the numerous bridges you will cross. The trail parallels the river along the south side between bluffs and trees with few stretches of open country. The many bridges tell the rider there are a lot of small gorges and feeder streams which empty into the Cannon River.

If you plan to ride both ways on your day, we recommend starting at Red Wing where there is a parking lot near the beginning of the trail just off old West Main St. This gives you an opportunity to explore Red Wing with its old river-town flavor. It also gives you the benefit of the slight downhill grade on the last half of the trip, rather than the first half. Along the way, you will find picnic tables about 3½ miles east of Cannon Falls, and portable restrooms at approximately 1/3 distance intervals. Refreshments in the village of Welch are available if you wish to take a short side trip.

A daily or seasonal "wheelpass" is required for trail use. They are available at self-purchasing stations at major access points, from merchants in Red Wing and Cannon Falls, or you may encounter an attendant along the trail.

A wheel pass is for users 16 or older and refers to anything with wheels: bicycles, rollerblades, skateboards, etc. To purchase by mail, write Cannon Valley Trail Headquarters, City Hall, Cannon Falls, MN 55009; by phone 507-263-3954.

CANNON FALLS

Administered by a Joint Powers Board from
Cannon Falls, Red Wing and Goodhue County.

14

Legend

➤	Mileage
π	Picnic
P	Parking
W	Water
R	Restrooms

Trail length: 12.5 miles

Surface: Blacktop

Access includes three separate parking lots with rest facilities.

Trailhead south: About 2 miles NW of Rochester on Co. Rd. 4, or if you are driving on Hwy. 52 take the IBM exit west to Co. Rd. 4. There is ample paved parking, shelter and portable restrooms.

In the area: Rochester has many areas of interest including the Mayo Clinic and Museum, Mayowood and the 30,000 giant Canada geese that live at Silver Lake Park. Bring a bag of bread and wear shoes. You can write or call for more information:

> Rochester Visitors Bureau
> 220 South Broadway, Suite 100
> Rochester MN 55902
> 800-426-6025

Mid access: Douglas on Co. Rd. 14 exit off Hwy. 52. There is a large parking lot, shelter, water and restrooms at milepost 5 from Rochester.

Trailhead north: Pine Island Park on the NE corner of Pine Island just south of exit from Hwy. 52. Parking, restrooms, water and picnic tables.

The Douglas Trail is one of the few in the state that can be covered in its entirety, riding both directions, in less than four hours. Its 12½ mile length combined with easy access and adequate parking at both trailheads make this an excellent half-day, one vehicle trip.

Enroute you will cross the Zumbro River and Plum Creek on wide, refurbished bridges. The trail itself is wide and in excellent condition with the only hazard being the need to cross several country gravel roads. The trail winds past a golf course and through fertile farm country. It is not heavily wooded but there is tree cover much of the way. You may encounter horseback riders as a horse and cross-country ski trail parallel the bike path and the two cross at occasional, well-marked points.

There is an interesting country store adjacent to the trail at Douglas, as well as good drinking water out of an old-fashioned hand pump located near the trail. This is also an excellent access point with parking lot.

This is a good choice for an early or late season ride when that unusually nice day comes along, but we recommend it at any time during the biking season.

Bike Shorts

• Check your tire pressure every week. Keep your tires inflated to the pressure on the side of the tire. Always check your tires before a trail ride.

• You should have a bell or a horn to alert pedestrians and other riders when passing on the left side of the trail.

ZUMBRO LAKE

Zumbro

⑫

ONOCO

Middle

Fork

River

52

Zumbro

River

63

Fork

➤ Mileage
π Picnic
P Parking
W Water
S Shelter
R Restrooms
■ Rest Areas

South

Administered by Minnesota Department
of Natural Resources

P
S R

㉒

ROCHESTER

Trail length: 28 miles

Surface: Blacktop

Trailhead west: The trail begins at
Heartland Park in Park Rapids. Going east
on Hwy. 34 through Park Rapids, you turn
north on Central Avenue. There is a sign on
Central Avenue indicating the Heartland
Trail. You turn left (west) on North Street which leads right
into the park. There is a large paved lot with excellent
facilities and you may park there overnight.

In the area: Itasca State Park is just 21 miles north of Park
Rapids. There are 17 miles of bike paths in the park. (page 46)

> Itasca State Park
> Lake Itasca MN 56460
> 218-266-3656
> 800-765-CAMP (2267) for accommodations.

Trailhead east: In Walker where Hwy. 34 intersects with Co.
Rd. 12. The trailhead is 3/4 mile west on Co. Rd. 12. The
parking lot with restrooms is set back from the street.

In the area: Leech Lake is located in Minnesota's heartland in
the Chippewa National Forest. For other tourist information,
write:

> Walker Leech Lake
> Walker Chamber of Commerce
> Walker MN 56484
> MN 800-247-0944

If you enjoy the north woods, glacial lakes and flowing
streams, you will like the Heartland Trail. The west trailhead
is located just 21 miles from one of the major attractions in
northern Minnesota, the Itasca State Park and the origin of
the mighty Mississippi River.

Paved in 1975, this was the first black-topped trail in Minnesota, perhaps in the country. The Heartland is a popular trail for snowmobilers in winter. The surfaced bike portion is part of many miles of trail for winter recreation which are not suitable for biking except for the real mountain bike enthusiasts. These trails do, however, offer an opportunity to get off your bicycle and just take a quiet walk in the woods.

The 28 miles of paved bike trail is an easy one-half day ride through the Chippewa State Forest and also lends itself to a two-way, one day ride. Our group prefers to ride to Walker one day and back to Park Rapids the next. This is partly because of the driving distance from home, but also because of the interesting towns, scenery, and the area in general. For overnight trips, reservations are highly recommended if you want a motel room during the tourist season.

If you plan to ride two half-days, we recommend starting at Heartland Park in Park Rapids where you may leave your car overnight. Heading east out of Park Rapids you will soon find yourself in deep woods with only an occasional farm field or residence in sight. 10.5 miles brings you into Nevis where we had lunch at a most unusual restaurant.

Another 5.5 miles puts you in Akeley where you will want to ride the one block off the trail and have your picture taken while sitting on the hand of a huge Paul Bunyan statue at the municipal park on Main St. On the north side of the trail at Akeley, there is a picnic shelter, tables and outdoor restrooms. A well with hand pump will give you good water.

From Akeley to Walker is probably the most scenic section. You leave the proximity of Highway 34 (and its occasional residence) and ride by numerous lakes. The east end of the trail ends rather abruptly and it is necessary to ride the last 1/4 mile into Walker on city streets.

In Walker we found excellent accommodations at reasonable rates with a good family restaurant just a short distance from the marina on beautiful Leech Lake.

Administered by Minnesota Department of Natural Resources

> Mileage
π Picnic
P Parking
W Water
S Shelter
R Restrooms

Trail length: 30 miles

Surface: Crushed limestone

Trailhead east: From I-494 exit west on Hwy. 12 (Wayzata Blvd.) to Co. Rd. 15 (Gleason Lake Rd.). Turn north and exit to the north on Vicksburg Lane. Continue north to 10th Ave. N. (there is a sign) and turn west 1/2 block to the parking lot with restrooms.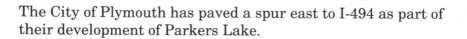

The City of Plymouth has paved a spur east to I-494 as part of their development of Parkers Lake.

If you are traveling west on Hwy. 55, west of I-494, turn south at Vicksburg Lane.

Mid access: Several county roads cross the trail but the only interim parking lot is at Stubbs Bay Rd. in Orono. You can access at Watertown where the trail crosses Co. Rd. 24. Street parking only.

In the area: Lake Minnetonka and the western suburbs as well as the entire Twin Cities area. More information on attractions in the area is available from:

>Twin West Chamber of Commerce
>10550 Wayzata Blvd. #2
>Minnetonka MN 55343
>612-540-0234

Trailhead west: The limestone surface actually ends at Co. Rd. 9 in Winsted but the parking lot is a short distance east on Lake Winsted. There is a county park with facilities at the southern tip of Lake Winsted.

The Luce Line Trail actually begins at the parking lot on 10th Ave. N. just off Vicksburg Lane, but the City of Plymouth paved a short section east to I-494. The DNR trail has a firm crushed limestone and well-maintained surface that extends 30 miles west to Winsted.

Through the foresight of the Luce Line Trail Association and subsequently the State Legislature, the right of way continues west from Plymouth for 97 miles, just 55 miles short of the South Dakota border. Think of the ride it will make when complete! Mountain bikes are now able to negotiate much more of this trail than touring or racing bikes. From Winsted west there are bridges to be replaced or built and the trail evaporates for short stretches, principally in villages and towns.

Thirty miles may necessitate a two vehicle outing unless you want to make it a long trip or take only a portion of the trail. The majority of the distance is through open country with only scattered tree cover except in the Wayzata-Plymouth end. The eastern 8 or 10 miles is really the most interesting with residential sections, trees, lakes and a different view when you ride through the Wayzata Country Club.

We prefer to start at the east end but wind direction may be a consideration because it is a fairly open trail for much of the route. Although there are few towns, Lyndale is an interesting stop for refreshments. Be sure your water bottle is full and you have snacks in your pack for this trail.

Administered by Minnesota Department of Natural Resources

➤ Mileage
π Picnic
P Parking
R Restrooms

Carlton to West Duluth Segment

Trail length: 14.5 miles

Surface: Blacktop

Trailhead north: Driving north on I-35 take Cody St. exit
(251A). Turn right on 63rd driving south (right); you will
intersect with Grand Avenue. The trailhead is right across the
street from the Lake Superior Zoological Garden at 72nd
Avenue West and Grand Avenue. Turn left to parking lot near
Willard Motel.

In the area: There are many reasons to visit Duluth. Exit
I-35 at the Spirit Mt. ramp and stop at the State Information
Center or call:

> Duluth Visitors Bureau
> 1-800-4-DULUTH

Trailhead west: Exit from I-35 on Hwy. 210, drive east to
Carlton. At the four-way stop turn onto Co. Rd. 1 and proceed
about one block to the trailhead parking lot.

In the area: For information on Jay Cooke State Park, call
800-862-2370

Driving south on I-35, take Grand Ave. exit (S23).

The Carlton to West Duluth segment is the very northern 14.5 miles of what is eventually planned to be a single trail from St. Paul to Duluth (and perhaps beyond). When they complete the 25 to 30 miles between this and the Hinckley trail at Barnum what a super distance ride it will make.

The first time we selected this trail, we started at Duluth. 14.5 miles makes an easy two-way ride but the first 9 miles seem more of a grade than the 3% slope and we wanted to do that part while we were still fresh. We recommend this approach for that reason and because it permits you to start and end your ride in Duluth. While the ride up is a bit strenuous, the long coast back down makes up for it.

Along the way, there are some interesting cuts through solid rock, a great view of Lake Superior and Wisconsin, and other scenic vistas. The trail takes you through woods, along-side Jay Cooke State Park and over a high bridge overlooking a spectacular gorge where you may see park visitors swimming and fishing. We did not join them, but not much further west, we did cool off by wading into a cool, clear stream paralleling our path.

One pleasant surprise enroute was a mobile refreshment stand run by an enterprising individual complete with ice cream, pop, candy, food and picnic tables.

If you choose a one-way ride, there is ample parking one block from downtown in Carlton. Because of the long down grade, you will find the Carlton to Duluth ride will take quite a bit less time so you may want to include a side trip into Jay Cooke State Park.

Carlton to West Duluth Segment

Administered by Minnesota Department of Natural Resources

DULUTH

2

ELDES
RNER

23

Spirit
Lake

SUPERIOR

Fond
du Lac   23 39

P Parking

31

Gateway Segment

Trail length: 16.9 miles

Surface: Blacktop

Trailhead west: Take the Maryland exit off
I35E just north of downtown St. Paul. Go east one block to
Westminster Ave., turn north to Arlington Ave. It is about ½
block west on Arlington to a paved parking lot on the south
side of the street. Portable toilets possible.

Mid access: The trail is accessible from a number of streets
and city parks.

Phalen-Keller Regional Park has parking available and you
can add 2.9 miles of paved trail. See Map, page 65.

In Maplewood, Flicek Park on Frost Avenue has parking
available.

Near the junction of Hwy. 36 and I694 in Oakdale, there is
a paved parking lot and portable toilets. From Hwy. 36 go
south ¼ block on Hadley Avenue to 55th St. North. Go east on
55th St. ½ mile to parking area on right.

In Pine Springs, from Hwy. 36, go north on Hilton Ave., and
take first right onto High Trail Avenue North. Parking is
available in the cul-de-sac.

There is a parking lot on the south side of Hwy. 96, just
west of the intersection of Hwy. 96 and Kimbro Avenue North.

Trailhead east: Although the trail continues a short distance
east (not paved), the best access and parking is at Pine Point
Park. Approximately five miles north of Stillwater on Hwy. 55
(Norell Ave. N.), on the west side of the road. Washington
County charges a fee for parking. Portable toilets.

The Gateway Trail represents the third and most recent addition to the Willard Munger State Trail. (See Hinckley Fire and Carlton-Duluth.) Its wide surface, easy access and excellent parking facilities provide a first class trail with more side trip options than most. The metropolitan location, especially the west 7.2 miles, make it one of the more popular multi-use trails. Expect more than the usual amount of foot, skater and wheelchair traffic on the western half.

You will find this to be a ride of contrasts. The west half winds through concentrated residential sections, along or through city parks and golf courses and crosses some busy streets. The eastern half passes through more open country, light traffic roads and lighter trail use. You may encounter horseback riders as the DNR has included a riding path paralleling the bike trail on the section north of I-694.

At just under 17 miles, this is a good trail for a ride both ways in one day. There are many opportunities for side trips to lengthen your ride. Phalen-Keller Regional Park has 2.9 miles of paved trail. You can ride either west to Mahtomedi or east to Stillwater on the paved Washington County trail that intersects with the Gateway at Washington County #12. When you reach Pine Point Park you will see a Washington County paved trail along #55 (Norell Ave.) both north and south for several miles.

Excellent bridges with no more than a 5% grade take you up and over two of the busiest streets (McKnight and White Bear). Expect to cross numerous city streets and a few county roads. Also, note a darker than usual surface on sections of this trail. The DNR is experimenting with a surface of shredded junk tires and pulverized shingles as aggregate mix rather than gravel in the bituminous. Both the DOT and the DNR are still evaluating its possibilities.

Worthy of note—Although the trail is in a large population area, we saw almost no opportunity for refreshments or rest room facilities within reasonable distance along the entire trail except for those provided by the DNR.

Gateway Segment

White Bear Lake

35E

WHITE BEAR
LAKE

P
SPR

61

694

Silver
Lake

LITTLE
CANADA

MAPLEWOOD

NORT
ST. PA

Robin
Hood
Park

36

Keller
Regional Park

Flicek
Park

35E

Lake
Como

Lake Phalen
Regional Park

Lake
Phalen

ST. PAUL

Carnelian Junction

Big Carnelian Lake

Pine Point Park

Loon Lake

Silver Lake

Little Carnelian Lake

95

55

96

Duluth Junction

MAHTOMEDI

15

Woodpile Lake

12

STILL-WATER

St. Croix River

S

36

Lake De Montreville

Paved trail (16.9 miles)

City or county park

Parking lot

Lake Olson

Lake Jane

5

4

N

Administered by Minnesota
Department of Natural Resources

0   1   2   3 Miles

35

Hinckley Fire Trail Segment

Trail length: 36.5 miles,
Hinckley to Barnum

Surface: Blacktop

Trailhead south: Exit I-35 at Hinckley and go west to old
Hwy. 61. Turn north and continue to Co. Rd. 18, turn west
across the tracks to parking lot with facilities on the
Grindstone River.

In the area: The Hinckley Fire Museum, the story of an era,
its people and a fire. The Mission Creek 1894 Theme Park and
Tobie's restaurant are on the east side of I-35.

Trailheads north: At Moose Lake, exit I-35 at Co. Rd. 27.
Drive one mile west to Hwy. 61, then south one block to
parking lot.

The trailhead at Barnum is on Co. Rd. 6 on the north side of
town.

Bike Shorts

• The most certain way to ride regularly is to develop a
group of interested friends.

• Always carry your own water bottle. For a cool drink,
fill your water bottle the night before and freeze overnight.

The Hinckley Fire Trail obviously got its name from the forest fire of 1894. This catastrophe of many years ago adds considerable interest to this ride. The trail is laid upon a rail bed which played an important role during the fire. While in Hinckley you will want to save some time to visit the Hinckley Fire Museum near downtown.

Heading north from Hinckley, you will find scattered forest or trees with considerable farm land. It is very flat with only an occasional grade except for a short, curvy stretch where they left the rail bed. This is one of the more open routes and you may want to consider wind direction when planning your trip.

Should you choose to access at a point other than the trailheads, Finlayson, Willow River and Sturgeon Lake are all easy to get to. The bikeway stretches 36.5 miles between Hinckley and Barnum and will someday connect to the Willard Munger Trail at Carlton.

If you want a 3 to 5 hour ride for your day's exercise, it will be necessary to leave a car at either end or make it an overnight stay. Good motels are available at both Moose Lake and Hinckley.

Bike Shorts

- There are 570 miles of off-road bikeways in Minnesota.

- Keep brakes, horn and other safety devices in good working condition. Brakes should be able to make the wheel skid on a dry, clean surface. Inspect your bike often for needed repairs/worn out parts.

Hinckley Fire Trail Segment

BARNUM

4.5 mi.

MOOSE LAKE

73 27

P

6 mi.

STURGEON LAKE

46

Sturgeon Lake

4 mi.

Willow River

WILLOW RIVER

P

41

43

Pine River

RUTLEDGE

4.3 mi.

23

5.5 mi.

P

FINLAYSON

3.5 mi.

ASKOV

GRONINGEN

SANDSTONE

4.5 mi.

61

FRIESLAND

North Fork Grindstone

61

35

Kelly River

20

4 mi.

HINCKLEY

18

R P

48

➤ Mileage
P Parking
R Restrooms

Administered by Minnesota
Department of Natural Resources

38

Trail length: 31 miles

Surface: Blacktop

Trailhead west: Now located one mile east of Fountain on the south side of Co. Rd. 8. Parking and portable restrooms available. Trail extension into Fountain is in the planning stage.

Mid access: At Whalen — permanent restrooms, picnic tables. At Lanesboro — the trail passes through the center of town crossing Co. Rd. 250.

Access at Isinours Unit on Co. Rd. 17. The parking lot is about 1/4 mile west of Co. Rd. 17 at Isinours wood lot.

In the area: Lanesboro is a picturesque village with antique shops, a winery, campground, a historic inn and two bed and breakfast inns. An eatery on the main street has live music and wonderful food. There is a resident wood carver and Amish gift shop.

Trailhead east: Rushford's main thoroughfare is Mill St., also marked Hwy. 43. The trailhead is one block west, just past Hwy. 16 and before Hwy. 30. The depot is open year around and is being developed into a railroad and trail museum.

For information on this charming area call or write for a brochure.
       Historic Bluff Country
       P.O. Box 609, Harmony MN 55939
       507-886-2230

Completed in 1989, The Root River Trail provides 31 paved miles along the Root River valley and through the hardwood forest and bluffs of this historic region. Consider it for an early or late season ride, but it is great any time of the year. It is one of the more level trails except at the extreme west end and a short adjustment about mid-point between Fountain and Lanesboro.

The 31 miles makes it an ideal one-way ride for the casual bicyclist, but the opportunities and attractions of this general area suggest an overnight stay at one of the several bed and breakfasts or motels along or near it. Try riding both ways on a two day excursion.

The Root River State Trail follows the watershed and general route of the south branch of its namesake between Fountain and Lanesboro and joins the main branch just east of Lanesboro. Although the trail is not always adjacent to a river, you will often see trout fisherman, canoeists and other outdoor enthusiasts on your ride. The trail includes 48 bridges with lengths of up to 500 feet. Of course, the towns of Fountain, Lanesboro and Rushford are attractions in themselves, with the entire downtown section of Lanesboro listed on the National Register of Historic Places.

The route will take you through the scenic bluffs and extensive hardwood forest of southern Minnesota. Be alert for wildlife, especially through the Lost Lake Game Refuge just west of Lanesboro. Worthwhile side trips include the State Fish Hatchery south of Lanesboro on Highway 16 or the Amish Community and shops at Harmony.

We prefer to plan this trip for a one-way ride from the west trailhead just east of Fountain to the east trailhead near downtown Rushford. The main reason is that it gives you a downhill ride all the way with one exception when the trail leaves the valley to get on top of the bluffs and return to the rail bed after a short distance.

At Fountain, there is ample parking, a shelter and portable restrooms. From this point, the trail takes an immediate downhill grade for nearly two miles until it reaches the river valley. Three miles further along you will see an old railroad building and another parking lot. This was once the point where the railroad used to put on a second engine to pull the trains up the grade you just came down. It is also the site of the Isinours Demonstration Woodland where you may want to take a walking side trip and view the many varieties of trees (labeled) with which the foresters are experimenting or are observing.

In Lanesboro, you will ride by the dam which provides electricity for the city. The trail center is located in the basement of the Lanesboro Historical Society Museum. (Clean restrooms, water, trail maps, etc.) In fact, you will ride right through the downtown section which will provide all conveniences including parking and a nearby campground should you decide to start your trip there.

Heading east, your next stop might be Whalen where they conveniently provide picnic tables and restrooms at trailside. Your next chance for refreshments is Peterson, 9 miles further east. Nearing Rushford is the only part of the trip in open country or paralleling a highway. Once in Rushford, you will find ample parking near the depot and excellent restaurants and accommodations.

If your party has chosen to drop a vehicle at both trailheads to permit a one-way ride, take Hwy. 8 from Fountain to Lanesboro and then Hwy. 16 from Lanesboro to Rushford. However you do it, this is a ride you will want to do again and again.

43
RUSHFORD
Trail
Center
30
5 mi.
π
Root River
R.P.
16
25
105
16
SOUTH RUSHFORD
5 mi.
PETERSON
π
16
106
43
25
π
4 mi.
π

➤ Mileage
π Picnic
P Parking
S Shelter
R Restrooms

N

WHALAN
P R π
106

23

21

Administered by Minnesota Department of Natural Resources

43

Trail length: 39 miles

Surface: Crushed limestone

Trailhead west: North of Mankato on Hwy.
22 to Lime Valley Rd., (about) one mile north
of Hwy. 22 interchange on Hwy. 14 bypass.
Exit west off Hwy. 22. Parking but no facilities.

In the area: Located on the banks of the Minnesota River,
Mankato is the home of Mankato State University. Minneopa
Falls in Minneopa State Park is 5 miles west on Hwy. 68 and
U.S. 169. You can request information from:

> Mankato Chamber of Commerce
> P.O. Box 999
> Mankato MN 56002
> 507-345-4519

> Minneopa State Park
> Route 9, Box 143
> Mankato MN 56001
> 507-625-4388

Mid access: At Elysian on Hwy. 60. Parking lot with new
building and restrooms. At Waterville, Hwy. 13 and Hwy. 60.

Trailhead east: Exit I-35 at Hwy. 60. Trail begins on north
side of Hwy. 60 just west of restaurant.

In the area: The Ivan Willock Woodcarving Studio and School
is located in Faribault as are Shattuck School, the Faribault
Alexander House and the Rice County Historical Society. More
information is available from:

> Faribault Chamber of Commerce
> P.O. Box 434
> Faribault MN 55021
> 507-334-4381

A crushed limestone trail, Sakatah Singing Hills traverses part of three counties along its 39 miles. This level trail wanders near lush pastures and farmland, along several lakes, through three small towns and a forested state park. There are swimming beaches within a short ride off the trail at Sakatah Lake State Park, Waterville, Elysian, Madison Lake, and Cannon Lake. The fish hatchery in Waterville is open to visitors.

As yet, the trail has relatively few improvements such as picnic tables and rest stops, but with the several small towns and Sakatah State Park, restrooms and water are not hard to come by.

Thirty nine miles makes a pretty good one day ride so you may want to leave a car at Faribault if the wind is westerly, or at Mankato if the wind is easterly.

If you are campers as well as bikers, Sakatah State Park is 14 miles from the Faribault trailhead. In our group opinion, the east 14 miles is the most scenic as well as the most shaded and would make an excellent two way ride.

One should consider the lakeside town of Elysian as a starting point for both portions of the trail. It is very near the half-way point and has an excellent parking lot and shelter with restrooms and water.

35

11 **FARIBAULT**

38

Cedar L.

Well L.

12

13

Carmon Lake

P

WARSAW

18

15

14 mi

Tetonka Lake

Sakatah Lake

WATERVILLE

MORRISTOWN

SAKATAH LAKE
STATE PARK

60

16

.5 mile severance

13

➤ Mileage
P Parking
■ Rest Areas

N

WASECA

Administered by Minnesota
Department of Natural Resources

MINNESOTA

State Parks

Regional Parks

Hennepin Parks

Minneapolis
Parks and Recreation

St. Paul
Parks and Recreation

Many state and regional parks provide excellent bike paths as a part of their facilities. Although often short, they are well worth considering as a part of your family outing or for a short ride any time.

Minnesota has 65 state parks. Eleven provide designated bike paths as listed below.

Afton — From St. Paul, go 8 miles east on I-94, then 7 miles south on Co. Rd. 15, 3 miles east on Co. Rd. 20
4 mile bike path

Camden — On State Highway 23, ten miles south of Marshall
4 mile bike path

Ft. Snelling — Take Post Rd. off State Hwy. 5
5 mile bike path

Itasca — 21 miles north of Park Rapids on U.S. Hwy. 71
17 mile bike path (detailed description on page 52)

Lake Bemidji — 1.7 miles off old U.S. 71 on State Hwy. 20
1 mile bike path

Minneopa — 5 miles west of Mankato on State Hwy. 68 and U.S. 169
4 mile bike path

Minnesota Valley — Off U.S. Hwy. 169 west of Jordon
4 mile bike path

St. Croix — 16 miles east of Hinckley on State Hwy. 48
6.5 mile bike path

Sakatah — 14 miles west of Faribault on Hwy. 60
The Sakatah Singing Hills State Trail passes through the park (see page 44).

Sibley —   15 miles north of Willmar on U.S. Hwy. 71
5 mile bike path

William O'Brien —   State Hwy. 95, two miles north of Marine-
-on-St. Croix
2 mile bike path

This information is from *Minnesota State Parks - Naturally*
available from the Department of Natural Resources
Information Center, 500 Lafayette Road, St. Paul, MN 55155.
The Center is open Monday through Friday 8:00 a.m. to 4:30
p.m. You can visit the Information Center or order by mail.
Telephone in Minnesota toll free 800-766-6000.

ITASCA STATE PARK

Trail length: 17 miles

Surface: Paved

Here is a chance to combine a really scenic
bike ride with a visit to one of the more famous
state parks in the nation. Not only is the scenery impressive,
but the park offers a wide variety of other attractions. In
1991 this park celebrated its 100th birthday.

The off-road bike path is only 6.5 miles, with an additional 10.5
miles designated on low traffic roads. **Bike rentals are
available in the park.** The south trailhead starts at the
information center on the east entrance road, and the north
trailhead starts in the parking lot for the interpretive center at
the headwaters of the Mississippi River near the north
entrance road.

The location lends itself well to a companion trip with the
Heartland Trail (see page 18). Biking enthusiasts may want to
consider staying in Park Rapids or riding to Park Rapids. It is
only 20 miles via U.S. Highway 71 from the south edge of the
park. The highway has paved shoulders specifically marked
for biking or hiking and it would be an interesting ride.

The virgin pines, lakes and other attractions of the park make
this trail a real gem for the outdoor enthusiast and nature lover.
Be sure of your reservations, including campgrounds, during the
summer season. For reservations as well as general information
about the park contact:

> Itasca State Park Manager
> Lake Itasca MN 56460
> 218-266-3654
> 800-765-2267

Mississippi R.

P

P

Mississippi River
Headwaters
Interpretive Tours
Programs –Trails
Gifts

P

P

200

Itasca
Wilderness
Sanctuary

Lake Itasca

Bicycle
Rental

East Arm

38

N

P Parking

Schoolcraft

Elk
Lake

P

Douglas
Lodge

P

Forest Inn
Visitor Center

48

1

Mary L.

The Metropolitan Council publishes a comprehensive map and guide to regional parks in the following seven counties: Carver, Dakota, Hennepin, Ramsey, Washington, Anoka and Wright.

Of the parks detailed in the guide, the following have designated biking paths:

	map page
Bunker	55
Baker	56
Carver	57
Cleary Lake	58
Elm Creek	59
Hyland-Bush-Anderson	60
Lake Rebecca	61
North Hennepin Corridor	62
Grand Rounds	63
Central Mississippi Waterfront	63
Mississippi Gorge	63
Nokomis-Hiawatha	63
Minneapolis Chain of Lakes	63
Theodore Wirth	63
Minnehaha Pkwy	63
Como	64
Crosby Farm/Hidden Falls	64
Phalen	65

Anoka County Riverfront
Long Lake
Lake Elmo
Battle Creek
Rice Creek West

Detailed maps unavailable. See publication below.

This publication *A Map and Guide to Regional Parks in the Twin Cities Area* is available free of charge.

Metropolitan Council
230 East Fifth Street
St. Paul MN 55101
612-291-6359

Bunker Hills Regional Park
Hennepin County Park Reserve District (Anoka)
Trail Length — 5.5 miles, paved

Baker Park Reserve
Trail Length — 6.2 miles, paved

Located approximately 20 miles west of downtown Minneapolis on County Road 19, between Highway 12 and Highway 55. From Highway 12, take County Road 29 north to County Road 19, and follow 19 north to the main park entrance. From Highway 55, take County Road 24 west to County Road 19, turn south and follow 19 to the main park entrance, or take Highway 55 to County Road 19, turn south and follow 19 to the main entrance. Phone: 479-2258 (Gate) or 476-4666 (Office)

Carver Park Reserve

Trail Length — 7.65 miles, paved

Located in Victoria, on Carver County Road 11. Take Highway 7 west from Minneapolis and turn left on County Road 11. Or take Highway 5 west from Minneapolis and turn right on County Road 11.
Phone: 446-9474 (Gate) or 472-4911 (Nature Center)

Cleary Lake Regional Park
Trail Length — 3.5 miles, paved

Located near Prior Lake on Scott County Road 27. From Interstate 35W, go west on County Road 42, then south on County Road 27. Or take Interstate 494 to County Road 18, go south on 18 to Highway 101, then east to Highway 13, south on 13 to County Road 42, east on 42 to County Road 27, and south on 27 to the park entrance.
Phone: 447-2171 (Visitor Center)

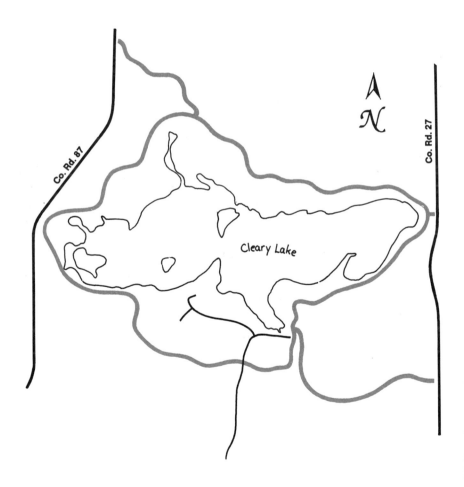

Elm Creek Park Reserve

Trail Length — 9.3 miles, paved (Also a 6.5 mile paved North Hennepin Trail corridor connects the Elm Creek trails with the Coon Rapids Dam.)

Located northwest of Osseo, between the communities of Champlin, Dayton and Maple Grove. For the recreation area, take County Road 81 to Territorial Road. Turn right and follow to the park entrance.
Phone: 424-5511 (Visitor Center)

A 5-mile turf trail is open for mountain biking; the designated mountain bike trail is the *only* turf trail where bikes are permitted.

Hyland Lake Park Reserve
Trail Length — 5.5 miles, paved

Located on East Bush Lake Road in Bloomington. From Interstate 494, go south on Normandale Blvd. (Highway 100) to 84th St. Turn right and follow 84th St. to East Bush Lake Road. Go south on East Bush Lake Road and follow the signs to Richardson Nature Center and Hyland Visitor Center. Phone: 941-4362

Lake Rebecca Park Reserve
Trail Length — 6.5 miles, paved

Located approximately 30 miles west of Minneapolis on
County Road 50. Take Highway 55 west to County Road 50,
turn left and follow to the park entrance.
Phone: 972-2620 (Trailhead)

North Hennepin Trail Corridor

Trail Length — 7.2 miles (also connects to the 9.3 mile Elm Creek trail), paved

Very flat trail connecting Elm Creek Park Reserve and Coon Rapids Dam Regional Park. Access from either park or several locations along the trail.

Grand Rounds Parkway System
Trail Length — 37.9 miles, paved

The system includes: the Chain of Lakes, Lake Nokomis, and Lake Hiawatha; Minnehaha, Shingle, and Bassett Creeks; and the Mississippi River.

Shingle Creek

Wirth Memorial Parkway

Mississippi River

Olson Hwy.

Theodore Wirth

Cedar

Franklin

Central Mississippi Waterfront

Lake Calhoun

Hennepin Ave.

Lake St.

Mississippi Gorge

Minnehaha Ave.

Hiawtha Ave.

Mississippi River

Mpls. Chain of Lakes

Lake Harriet

Minnehaha Pkwy.

Lake Nokomis

Nokomis - Hiawatha

Crosstown

Como Park
Trail Length — 1.8 miles, paved

Crosby Farm/Hidden Falls
Trail Length — 5 miles, paved

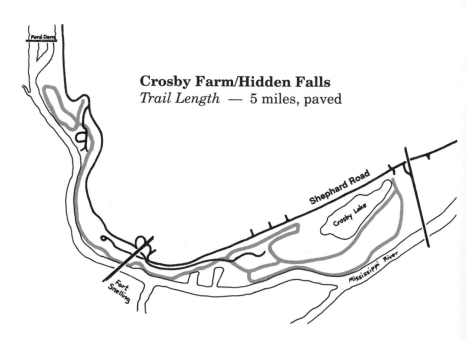

Phalen
Trail Length — 2.9 miles, paved

WESTERN WISCONSIN RAIL TRAILS

Red Cedar State Park Trail

Chippewa River State Park Trail

Great River State Park Trail

La Crosse River State Park Trail

Elroy-Sparta State Park Trail

The 400 State Trail

Many Wisconsin Trails are interconnected. The six included in this book are listed in the order of their proximity to each other.

Trail length: 14.5 miles

Surface: Crushed limestone

Trailhead north: On Hwy. 29 in west
Menominee at Riverside Park. Take second
exit west of Hwy. 29 bridge to renovated
depot.

Mid access: Irvington on Hwy. D (mile 2.7)
Downsville on Hwy. 25 (mile 7.5)
Dunnville on Hwy. Y (mile 12.5)

Trailhead south: Trail ends after crossing Chippewa River on
800 ft. trestle at junction with Chippewa River State Trail off
County Road M.

In the area: The Downsville Cooperative Creamery was
founded in 1904 and currently houses a restaurant, lounge,
four room inn, as well as showroom and shop for the Dunn
County Pottery.

For more information about the area, contact:

> Greater Menomonie Area
> Chamber of Commerce
> 335 Main Street
> P.O. Box 246
> Menomonie WI 54751
> 715-235-9087

We want to include the Red Cedar as one of our Vikingland trails, not only because it is the Wisconsin trail closest to the Twin Cities, but also because of its uniqueness and the many attractions of the area.

As with all Wisconsin trails, it is well-maintained crushed limestone. You will pass through woodlands and prairies and past unique rock formations. For most of its distance, the trail overlooks the Red Cedar River, also popular with canoeists. Several picnic tables have been provided in scenic spots where you can rest and relax.

Just after you cross the Chippewa River, you connect with the western end of the new Chippewa River Trail. We found the wide and sandy shores of the Chippewa to be an excellent picnic spot, plus you get the opportunity to ride perhaps the longest trestle (800 ft.) on any bike trail and enjoy a spectacular view in the process.

Since its total length is only 14.5 miles, it is a very manageable two-way ride no matter where you start. Give yourself some extra time for this one because there are so many interesting things to see and do along the way.

Bike Shorts

• Adults today are very health conscious and bicycling is one of the best forms of exercise.

• When you have children with you, take extra water.

Lake Memomin

MENOMONIE

IRVINGTON

2.7 ml.

π

D

P

4.8 ml.

π

Red Cedar River

25

E

J

Y

J

C

72

π P

DOWNSVILLE

C

RED CEDAR
TRAIL

π

π 7 ml.

Y

Chippewa

Ri

10 m

R

MER

O

Y

DUNNVILLE

25

M

N

➤ Mileage
π Picnic
P Parking
R Restrooms

Trail Length: 20 miles

Surface: Crushed limestone

Trailhead east: The trail begins in
downtown Eau Claire, First Avenue
along the Chippewa River. The first 3 or
4 miles are asphalt until you come to the
actual trailhead which is on the south city limits and the trail
becomes crushed limestone.

Mid Access: Meridean and Caryville

Trailhead west: Begins at south end of Red Cedar Trail,
south side of 800 ft. trestle crossing the Chippewa River off Co.
Rd. M.

   This trail is presently not open from Caryville to the
junction of Cedar River State Trail. (January 1993) Call
715-839-1607 for current developments.

GREAT RIVER STATE PARK TRAIL

Trail length: 24 miles

Surface: Crushed limestone

Trailhead north: South of Marshland, Wisc.
on Hwy 35, there is a parking lot that serves as the trailhead.
No facilities. The trail does not follow the rail bed until you
leave the wildlife refuge. About one mile down the trail you
have the option of taking the loop through the refuge. There is
no fee to use the trail through the refuge.

Mid access: Parking lots at Perrot State Park, Lytles, and
Midway. Near the city of Trempealeau there is a large parking
lot with portable toilets on Hwy. 35.

Trailhead south: The trail user leaves the trail and uses the
well marked bike route to get to the trailhead in the city of
Onalaska, Wisc. There is a brick building with restrooms and
a large paved parking lot. The trail ends before reaching the
LaCrosse River State Park Trail, but the user can follow a
marked bike route from that point.

In the area: Trempealeau National Wildlife Refuge, Perrot
State Park, Lock and Dam #6, the Upper Mississippi River
Wildlife and Fish Refuge and the scenic river valley and bluffs.

For a close-up look at waterfowl, wildlife, river bottoms and
bluffs, this Wisconsin Trail is an excellent choice. Generally
sheltered and shaded, it crosses two national refuges and 18
bridges including one that is 1226 feet long.

Because of the scenery, a side trip through Perrot State
Park and watching a tow lock through Lock & Dam #6, we
found this trail took a bit more time than its 24 miles would
indicate. Although riding both ways in one day is not
unreasonable, you may prefer a more leisurely trip for these

same reasons. We found overnighting in Trempealeau suited our schedule, riding south 14 miles and then back one afternoon, and north the 10 miles and back the next morning.

Eventually, this trail will connect to the LaCrosse River State Trail which now runs from LaCrosse to Sparta and ends just a short distance from the Elroy-Sparta Trail. The DNR Bureau of Parks and Recreation has some challenges in completing direct trail connections at the junctures. This is especially true of making a direct connection between the Great River and the LaCrosse River Trails in north LaCrosse. For now, you can make the connection by following the well placed bike trail signs from the Onalaska Trail Headquarters.

Bike Shorts

• Time your ride to avoid rush hour traffic. Midday on weekdays and weekends are the safest times to ride.

• "Done with indoor complaints, strong and content, I travel the open road."

—Walt Whitman

➤ Mileage
π Picnic
R Restrooms
P Parking
W Water

? Information: Center for Commerce & Tourism
471 2nd Ave. North (Hwy 35N)
Onalaska, WI 54650
(608) 781-9670

★ Trail Headquarters: Hilltopper & Oak Forest Drive
Exit 35N off I-90

0   1   2 Miles

Black

53

35

Amsterdam Prairie

NA
New Amsterdam

XX

Holmen

P R π W

P

10.8 mi.

Midway

53

Brice

Prairie

ZN

Z

35

3.2 mi.

er Wildlife and Fish Refuge

Lake Onelaska

Onalaska

?

La Crosse River State Trail

P   **W**
R **π**

★

North La Crosse

90

16

LACROSSE RIVER STATE PARK TRAIL

Trail length: 21.5 miles

Surface: Crushed limestone

Trailhead west: Exit Hwy. 16 East at stop
lights on Hwy. B intersection in north LaCrosse. Go
approximately ¼ mile on Hwy. B to Medary parking lot on left.

Mid-access: Hwy. 108 south of West Salem. Bangor and at
intersecting county roads.

Trailhead east: South edge of Sparta. Follow street signs to
renovated depot at South Water and Railroad St. in Sparta.
Ample parking and facilities in Sparta.

This is one of the newer rail trails in western Wisconsin and connects the Great River and Elroy-Sparta trails. Much of its 21.5 miles parallels the LaCrosse River and provides a variety of scenery including farmlands, hardwood forests and wetlands. It also parallels I-90 for much of the distance between N. LaCrosse and Sparta. There are some points where this detracts somewhat from the serenity of the ride. Its roadbed and bridges are in excellent condition and the length provides a challenging two-way ride or an easy one-way day trip.

Trail length: 32 miles

Surface: Crushed limestone

Trailhead west: Exit I-90 at Hwy. 27,
Sparta. Start at newly renovated
depot at S. Water and Railroad St.
(Also the east terminus of the LaCrosse State Trail.) Follow
well marked city streets south out of town to actual trailhead
on left of road where there is also parking and primitive
camping facilities.

Trailhead east: The west edge of Elroy just north of Hwy 71.
Three Wisconsin bike trails merge in Elroy where the city has
recently developed a downtown park with connections to each
trail. The Commons provide parking, restrooms, pay showers,
lockers, picnic facilities and even a "tot lot." Restaurants,
stores and the Elroy Area Historical Society are nearby.

Mid access: Norwalk on Hwy. 71 & Co. Rd. T (trail mile 11.9)
Wilton on Hwy. 71 & Co. Rd. M (trail mile 17.3)
Kendall on Hwy. 71 & Co. Rd. W (trail mile 26.4)
Trail headquarters is located at Kendall, 5.7 miles from east
trailhead.

In the area: Kendall's annual Labor Day weekend celebration
features a parade, dance, and plenty of barbecued chicken and
sweet corn.
    In Wilton the Lions Club serves pancake breakfasts in the
municipal park Sunday mornings from June to September.
    Sparta has a 34 acre lake.

The foresight of responsible individuals and the State of Wisconsin has provided us with a truly exceptional bike trail in an unusually scenic area. It has been maintained and in use since 1965 and has become well known nationally among biking enthusiasts.

The Elroy-Sparta Trail traverses the Hidden Valley country of Wisconsin providing spectacular scenery as well as great bird watching and possible wildlife sightings. (The entire trail is a wildlife refuge.) The area is heavily wooded, providing shelter from sun and wind. The woods also make this an extremely popular ride during the fall color season in the state.

The rugged and scenic attraction of the area probably tells you this trail is not the level or gradually inclined roadbed of the prairie or river bottom. In fact, there are few level stretches, with long, rather steep (for a railbed) inclines. The long upgrades are matched by equally long downgrades that give you the chance to rest up. This trail does, however, require more physical conditioning and stamina than most 32 mile rides.

There are three upgrades, each leading to a tunnel cut through solid rock. Those tunnels make the trail unique. Tunnel 3 (at mile 12.4 from west end) is .7 miles long. Tunnel 2 (at 19.5 miles) is .3 miles long and tunnel 1 (at mile 25.3) is .25 miles long. For tunnel 3, special equipment not taken along on most bike trips is highly recommended. A 3/4 mile tunnel is long and dark and you will need a flashlight. You may need an extra wrap as tunnels can be both cold and damp. You will need to walk your bike at least through tunnel 3, so it will take awhile. The spirit of adventure provided by the tunnels really adds something special to this trip.

In the valleys between each tunnel (as well as at each end) are interesting small towns that truly welcome bikers and provide food, refreshments and restrooms. Of special interest is the refurbished depot at Kendall which has been designated a national historic landmark. It also serves as the trail headquarters and as a railroad museum.

For the casual or weekend biker, a one-way trip is a full day ride. This necessitates staying overnight or dropping a car at one end. Should your party want to drop a car, Hwy. 71 parallels the trail all the way. If you have only one vehicle, this is one of the few trails that provides a driver service. Take two sets of keys with you and pick up a driver at the Kendall headquarters. The driver will drop you at your start point and return your car to Kendall. There is a nominal fee and reservations are recommended.

For further information contact:

Kendall Depot
Bike Trail Headquarters
P.O. Box 153
Kendall WI 54638
Phone 608-463-7109

Trail length: 22 miles

Surface: Crushed limestone

Trailhead north: The Commons in Elroy

Mid access: Union Center, Wonewoc, Lavalle

Trailhead south: Reedsburg

    A scenic ride paralleling the Baraboo River, includes ten river crossings as well as a number of feeder streams. The Baraboo is popular with canoeists and you may also encounter horseback riders because a horse trail runs alongside the 400 between Wonewoc and LaValle.

    This trail gets its name from a very well known passenger train of its day—the old Chicago Northwestern "400" from Chicago to the Twin Cities.

    Three Wisconsin bike trails merge in Elroy where the city has recently developed a downtown park with connections to each trail. The Commons provide parking, restrooms, pay showers, lockers, picnic facilities and even a "tot lot." Restaurants, stores and the Elroy Area Historical Society are nearby.

Juneau County
Omaha Trail

Elroy-Sparta
Trail

(71) ELROY

3.5 Miles

(80)(82)(33) UNION CENTER

3.5 Miles

Baraboo River

WONEWOC

(33)

Bicycle / Horse Trail Segment
7.5 Miles

Dutch Hollow
Lake

Lake
Redstone

LA VALLE

(33)

Baraboo

River

7.5 Miles

➤ Mileage
▲ Proposed trail rest area
O Proposed southern trail terminus
◇ Trail connectors

Babb Creek

REEDSBURG

83

MOUNTAIN BIKING
BIKING

MINNESOTA
WISCONSIN

Although the emphasis of this book is on the paved and/or maintained designated bicycle trails, it would not be complete without information on the fast growing sport of mountain biking.

Minnesota offers fat tire enthusiasts extensive opportunities to practice their off-road skills in its national forests and many of the state parks. Wisconsin also has a well marked and extensive mountain biking trail system. The growth of mountain biking generates continuing expansions of off-road areas in both states.

National Forests

Minnesota's national forests do not have trails specifically designated for off-road bicycle use, but allow bicycles on state forest roads and trails. A complete list of state forest trails is included in the booklet, "Minnesota State Forest Campgrounds and Recreation Areas," available from —

DNR Information Center
P.O. Box 40
500 Lafayette Rd.
St. Paul, MN 55146.
Phone: 612-296-6699, outstate MN 800-766-6000

Superior National Forest
(#20 on map)

Mountain biking is permitted on the gravel and dirt logging roads that wind through the woods, as well as on snowmobile and ski trails. The forest service has a brochure with a map of seven mountain bike trail loops. They range from easy gravel roads to rocky or swampy trails from about 10 miles to 22 miles long.

Several lodges along the Gunflint Trail offer bike rentals and lodge-to-lodge biking packages. For information, call 1-800-338-6932, the Gunflint Trail Association.

You may also contact—

Superior National Forest
PO Box 338
Duluth, MN 55801.
Phone 218-720-5324.

Mountain biking information and maps are available at the Superior National Forest ranger stations in Tofte and Grand Marais, both on Hwy. 61.

Giants Ridge Recreation Area
(#21 on map)

Giants Ridge opens its trails to mountain bikers May 15 through October. There are about 30 miles of mostly mowed grass, over steep, wooded hills that tie into the 120 miles of trails in the Superior National Forest. Each Labor Day weekend, Giants Ridge hosts a mountain bike fest. Giants Ridge is about 70 miles north of Duluth, near Biwabik. For more information contact—

Giants Ridge
Box 190
Biwabik, MN 55708
Phone: 218-865-4143

Chippewa National Forest
(#22 on map)

Mountain biking is currently permitted on hiking trails, snowmobiling and skiing trails, as well as logging roads in the Chippewa National Forest. Maps of the forest and its trails are available from ranger stations in Cass Lake, Walker, Deer River, Marcell and Blackduck. For information, contact Chippewa National Forest, Cass Lake, MN 56633, 218-335-8600.

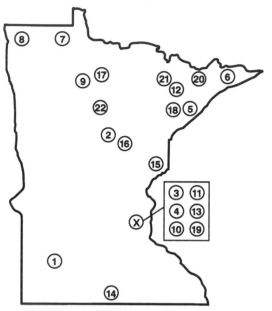

For more information on mountain biking in Minnesota state parks and forests, contact the DNR Information Center, 500 Lafayette Rd, Box 40, St. Paul, MN 55155, 612-296-6157. Outstate MN 800-766-6000. A complete list of state forest trails is included in the booklet, "Minnesota State Forest Campgrounds and Recreation Areas".

1992 Minnesota Off-Road (Mountain Biking) Trails

1	Camden State Park, Marshall	4.25
2	Cuyuna Country Proposed State Park	mileage unavailable
3	Elm Creek Park Reserve, Maple Grove	5
4	Ft. Snelling, Twin Cities	5
5	Gooseberry Falls State Park, Beaver Bay	10
6	Gunflint Trail, Grand Marais	140
7	Hayes Lake, Roseau	4
8	Lake Bronson, Lake Bronson	4
9	Lake Bemidji, Bemidji	5
10	Lebanon Hills Park, Eagan	2.5
11	Maplewood, Twin Cities	10.5
12	McCarthy Beach, Side Lake	12
13	Minnesota Valley Trail State Park, Jordan	35
14	Myre-Big Island, Albert Lea	7
15	St. Croix, Hinckley	23.5
16	Savanna Portage, Libby	10
17	Scenic, Big Fork	5
18	Split Rock Lighthouse, Beaver Bay	6
19	Sunfish Lake Park, Lake Elmo	mileage unavailable

This symbol is used in state parks to designate trails intended for use by off-road bicycles.

Trail Use Tips
• Respect the rights of other trail users. Always yield to hikers, horses and other animals.
• Pass with care to avoid startling other users.
• Stay on trails to preserve fragile ecosystems.
• Control your speed, especially on hills and around curves.
• Don't litter, put in proper place.
• Plan ahead for your own safety.
• Drug or alcohol use is prohibited.
• Camping and fires are not allowed.
• Be careful of poisonous plants.
• Don't feed the wild animals.
• Leave wild flowers alone. Do not pick!
• Never eat wild berries.
• Respect privately owned land adjacent to trail.

For more information on
mountain biking in
Wisconsin, contact
DNR Bureau of Parks
and Recreation
P.O. Box 7921
Madison, WI 53707

Phone 608-266-2181

1992 Wisconsin Off-Road (Mountain) Bicycle Trails

Park/Forest	Phone	Trail Name	Mileag
1 Black River	715-284-1400	Castle Mound	4.5
		Pigeon Creek	4
		Ski Trails	25
		Undesignated/unmarked trails, logging roads NOT posted against bicycle use.	
2 Blue Mound	608-437-5711	Pleasure Valley, Ridgeview, Walnut Hollow, Military Ridge Connector	4
3 Bong	414-878-5600	Hiking/ski trails north of 142 and east of B	
4 Brule River	715-372-4866	Ski trail	5.6
		Undesignated/unmarked trails,logging roads NOT posted against bicycle use.	15
5 Buffalo River	608-687-4936	Entire trail	36.4

Directions

1½ mi SE of Black River Falls on US 12
12 mi SE of Black River Falls on US 12, then 4 mi NE on
C.T.H. O and North Settlement Town Rd.

12 mi SE of Black River Falls on US 12, then 5 mi NE on C.T.H. O or
5 mi NE on North Settlement Town Rd.

Forest-wide

1 mi NW of Blue Mounds off US 18 and 151

8 mi SE of Burlington off Hwy. 142

2 mi NW of Brule on US 2, then 2 mi W on After Hours Rd.

From Fairchild to Mondovi via US 10

1992 Wisconsin Off-Road (Mountain) Bicycle Trails

Park/Forest	Phone	Trail Name	Mileag
6 Copper Falls	715-274-5123	Ski trails west of the main park entrance road	8.25
7 Council Grounds	*Summer:* 715-536-8773 *Off Season:* 715-536-4502	Hiking trail	2.5
8 Devil's Lake	608-356-8301	Ice Age Loop	4
		Steinke Basin	2.5
		East Bluff (connector)	1
9 Flambeau River	715-332-5271	Ski trails between Hwys. W and 70	14
		Undesignated/unmarked trails, logging roads NOT posted against bicycle use.	100
10 Governor Dodge	608-935-2315	Mill Creek	3.3
		Meadow Valley	6
11 Governor Knowles	715-463-2898	North hiking trail	9
		Undesignated/unmarked trails, logging roads NOT posted against bicycle use.	30
12 Harrington Beach	414-285-3015	Shuttle bus route/ski trail	2
13 Hartman Creek	715-258-2372	Bike trail connectors	1
14 High Cliff	414-989-1106	Snowmobile/horse	8.2
15 Kettle Moraine, N.U.	414-626-2116	New Fane	8
		Greenbush	11
16 Kettle Moraine, S.U.	414-594-2135	Emma Carlin	7.5
		John Muir	7.8
		Connector trail between Muir & Carlin	7.0
17 Kohler-Andrae	414-452-3457	Black River	2.5
18 Lake Wissota	715-382-4574	Horse trail	5
		Red Pine, fitness course, Eagle Prairie, & Jack Pine	6
19 Lapham Peak	414-646-3025	Hiking/ski trails	5

Directions

2 mi N of Mellen on Hwy. 169, then 2 mi on C.T.H. J

1 mi N of Merrill on Hwy. 107

3 mi S of Baraboo on Hwy. 123
3 mi S of Baraboo on Hwy. 123
3 mi S of Baraboo on Hwy. 123
18 mi W of Phillips on C.T.H. W

Forest-wide

3 mi N of Dodgeville on Hwy. 23
3 mi N of Dodgeville on Hwy. 23
15 mi N of Grantsburg off C.T.H. F
Forest-wide

10 mi N of Port Washington on I-43, then 1 mi E on C.T.H. D
6 mi W of Waupaca on Hwy. 54
3 mi S of Sherwood off Hwy. 55
4 mi NE of Kewaskum off County Line Rd.
2½ mi S of Greenbush off Kettle Moraine Dr.
3 mi W of Eagle on Hwy. 59, then ½ mi S on C.T.H. Z
5 mi S of Palmyra on C.T.H. H
Same as for Carlin & Muir trails

4 mi S of Sheboygan on I-43, 2 mi E on Park Dr.
8 mi NE of Chippewa Falls on Hwy. 29 & County Rd.
Same as Lake Wissota horse trails

2 mi S of Delafield off C.T.H. C

1992 Wisconsin Off-Road (Mountain) Bicycle Trails

Park/Forest	Phone	Trail Name	Mileag
20 Mirror Lake	608-254-2333	Trails south of Fern Dell Rd. (Beaver Pond, Fern Dell, Turtleville, Hastings, & Pioneer Loops)	9.2
21 Newport	414-854-2500	Trails south of Europe Bay Road & old farm maintenance road north of Europe Bay Road	12
22 Northern Highland-American Legion	715-356-5211	McNaughton Madeline Shannon Lumberjack	38 tota
		Undesignated/unmarked trails, logging roads NOT posted against bicycle use.	800
23 Pecatonica	608-523-4427	Calamine to Belmont	10
24 Peninsula	414-868-3258	Ski trails south of Middle Road	7
		Sunset Trail (surfaced limestone trail)	5.5
		Nicolet Bay to Tennison Bay Connector	.25
25 Perrot	608-534-6409	Ski trail & campground trail	8.5
26 Point Beach	414-794-7480	Red Pine	4
27 Potawatomi	414-746-2890	Ski trails	4
28 Tuscobia	715-266-3511	Entire trail	75
29 Wyalusing	608-996-2261	Mississippi Ridge	3.6
		Turkey Hollow	3.2
		Walnut Springs	0.6
		Whitetail Meadows	3.2

Directions

1½ mi SW of Lake Delton on Ishnala Rd.

3 mi E of Ellison Bay on Hwy. 42, then 2 mi SE on C.T.H. Z

12 mi NW of Rhinelander off Hwy. 47
2 mi N of Woodruff on US 51, then E 3 mi on Hwy. 70
4 mi SE of Sayner off C.T.H. G
9 mi NE of Boulder Jct. off C.T.H. B
Forest-wide

From Calamine to Belmont via C.T.H. G
¼ mi N of Fish Creek off Hwy. 42

Same as Peninsula Ski Trails

Same as Peninsula Ski Trails

2 mi NW of Trempealeau off Hwy. 35

4 mi N of Two Rivers off C.T.H. O
2 mi S of Sturgeon Bay on Hwy. 42 & 57
4 mi N of Rice Lake off US 53, then NE to Park Falls via Hwys. 48, 40, 70 and 13
7 mi S of Prairie du Chien on US 18, then W on C.T.H. C
Same as Wyalusing Mississippi Ridge Trail
Same as Wyalusing Mississippi Ridge Trail
Same as Wyalusing Mississippi Ridge Trail

1992 Wisconsin Off-Road (Mountain) Bicycle Trails

Park/Forest	Phone	Trail Name	Mileag
30 Chequamegon National Forest	715-762-2461	Rock Lake Flambeau Undesignated/unmarked trails, logging roads NOT posted against bicycle use.	13.5 55 250
31 Nicolet National Forest	715-362-3415	Anvil Ed's Lake Lauterman Undesignated/unmarked trails, logging roads NOT posted against bicycle use.	19 7 15 3,000
32 Lowes Creek	715-839-4738	Lowes Creek County Park bicycle/ski trail	4.9
33 Langlade Co. Forest	715-627-6236 or 800-288-6236	Jack Lake cross country ski trail Moccasin Lake Road cross country ski trail	14 6
34 Lincoln Co.	715-453-5334	Hiawatha	6.6
34 Lincoln Co. Forest	800-352-9602 715-536-0304	Underdown Recreation Trails	18
35 Nine-Mile County Forest Rec. Area	715-847-5267	Nine-Mile cross country ski & snowmobile trails	25
36 Oconto Co.	414-834-6820	Oconto County Recreation Trail	30
37 Racine Co.	414-886-8440	North ShoreTrail MRK Trail Burlington Trail Waterford-Wind Lake Trail	3 5 4 5
38 Rusk Co.	715-532-2113	Blue Hills Trail	12
39 Taylor Co.	715-748-4729	Pine Line	38
40 Winnebago Co.	414-424-0042	Larsen Trail Rush Lake Trail	14 5.3

TOTAL 1992 WISCONSIN OFF-ROAD (MOUNTAIN)

BICYCLE TRAIL MILEAGE 4,901.

Directions

7.5 mi E of Cable on C.T.H. M
5 mi E of Fifield on Hwy. 70
Forest-wide

8.5 mi E of Eagle River on Hwy. 70
2 mi E of Crandon on Hwy. 8, then 9 mi S on C.T.H. W
12 mi W of Florence on Hwy. 70 to Forest Rd 2154, then S ¼ mi
Forest-wide

State Hwy. 93 S of Eau Claire to C.T.H. S, then W 1¼ mi to Lowes Creek Rd., then S 1½ mi

12 mi N of Antigo on Hwy. 45, then E on C.T.H. J 2 mi to jct. of Pence Lake Rd. and road to Veterans Memorial Park

N of Antigo on Hwy. 45 to Elcho, then 2 mi W on Moccasin Lake Rd., then S ¼ mi on Bear Rd.

From Hwy. 51 take Hwy. 86 exit W to Tomahawk, then Somo Ave. W to Sara Park Activity Center.

Hwy. 51 N of Merrill to C.T.H. H, E 1 mi to Copper Lake Rd, then E 4 mi

From Wausau S on Hwy. 51 to C.T.H. N, then W 3.5 mi to Red Bud Rd., then 1.5 mi S

From US 41/141 take Hwy. 141 to Hwy. 22 W to Gillett.

Exit I-94 at Hwy. 20, then E 7 mi to West Blvd., then S to 19th Street

Exit I-94 at Seven Mile Rd., then E 7 mi

City of Burlington's Riverside Park located 3 blocks SE of Hwy. 36 off Maryland Ave.

1 mi NE of Waterford off Hwy. 20-83

8 mi NW of Village of Bruce to #2 Fire Lane, then 2.5 mi N

From Medford ½ mi N on Hwy. 13, then 1 mi W on Allman Street

From US 41 exit Hwy. 110 to Oshkosh, then turn right on West Wind Rd.

From Oshkosh W on Hwy. 21 to C.T.H. K, then S to Eureka, then S to Rush Lake on C.T.H. E, then left on Rush Loop

SAFETY
AND
EQUIPMENT

Fortunately, accidents and injury are not common in cycling, especially beyond the exuberance of youth. But they do happen and certainly detract from the enjoyment of a bike trip.

Common sense and awareness are the best policy. Even the most experienced among us can benefit from a periodic refresher course on the subject, so following are some safety tips that should be stored in everyone's memory bank:

Common Sense:
1. Obey traffic laws and obey traffic signs. Most serious accidents involve motor vehicles and drivers are conditioned to expect you to do as another motor vehicle would.

2. Go with the traffic flow, signal your turns and lane changes and be especially alert for pedestrians or car doors opening when passing a line of parked cars or other roadside obstructions. Stay as close to the right side of the road as possible.

3. Yield the right-of-way to vehicles or pedestrians. Be prepared to do so even if you have the right-of-way. A bicycle is hardly the vehicle for practicing that a good offense is the best defense.

4. Wear an approved helmet. This is one of the most important precautions you can take to avoid serious injury. (See Mayo Clinic article on the subject, page 102.)

5. Plan your ride so you are off the streets, roads and trails by dusk. Bicycles are best left parked or stored at night, but if you must, be sure you have front, side and rear reflectors, plus lights. Wear or switch to light-colored clothing.

6. Give an audible signal (we recommend a bike bell) before passing pedestrians or other cyclists.

Awareness:

1. Give your bike a pre-ride check. This is not only for maintenance. Good brakes and a mechanically sound bike are necessary for maximum safety and enjoyment. Check your tire pressure every week. Keep your tires inflated to the pressure noted on the side of the tire.

2. When planning a trip, be aware of your own capabilities as well as the limitations and health of your friends. A ride which tests one's outer limits is best left to those conditioned to do so.

3. Be alert to changing conditions. Rain will muffle the sound of approaching vehicles and generate slippery conditions, especially after a long period without rain. (Roadway oil and grime can be hazardous until the rain washes them away.)

4. Watch for road debris or loose rocks or gravel. Slow down if there is excessive debris or broken road surface. Learn to guide your bike very straight and vertical through loose sand or rocks. If you find a short stretch of loose sand it would even pay to practice riding through it a few times to give you needed confidence when it surprises you along the trail.

5. The old Irish prayer "May the wind blow always at your back" is only partially true for bicyclists. Be prepared for the vacuum effect of passing vehicles, sudden gusts or sudden absences when passing roadside buildings, trees or other shelter.

6. A word about dogs, many of whom seem to take particular objection to bicycles. If you encounter one, the first requirement is not to panic. If the dog is only testing, and not actually attacking, a shout or order may keep it at bay. If it is very aggressive, the best defense is to dismount, keeping the bike between you and the dog. Grab anything available to throw or pretend to throw. Most of all, keep moving as a dog is only going to defend what it perceives to be the limits of its territory.

Bicycle helmets*

Protective headgear can be a lifesaver

It's as easy as falling off a bicycle.

The adage has been around for decades. Unfortunately, it makes light of the potential for tragedy if you should take a serious fall while riding a bicycle.

With an increasing number of people riding bicycles on our streets and highways, the risk of injury — in particular, head injury — continues to rise. Each year, nearly 50,000 bicyclists suffer serious head injuries. According to the most recent statistics, head injuries are the leading cause of death in the approximately 1,300 bicycle-related fatalities that occur annually. To a large extent, these head injuries are preventable.

Wearing a helmet can make a difference

Until recently, advocates of the use of protective headgear for cyclists found their stance lacked scientific support. But wearing protective headgear clearly makes a difference. Recent evidence confirms that a helmet can reduce your risk of serious head and brain injury by almost 90 percent should you be involved in a bicycle accident.

Factors that can lead to head injury

Don't let common myths lull you into a false sense of security regarding your risk of head injury while riding a bicycle.

Myth: "Head injuries only happen to kids."
Fact: Only half of all brain and head injuries occur in teenagers and young children.

Myth: "I only ride in safe areas."
Fact: While most serious accidents involving bicycle riders occur on paved roads or bicycle paths, they even can occur on grass.

Myth: "I never ride fast enough to be injured."
Fact: Nearly half of all the accidents resulting in head and brain injuries caused no damage to the bicycle.

Bicycle riding is an excellent form of aerobic exercise that can benefit your musculoskeletal and cardiovascular systems. Make the investment in a helmet and take the time to put it on each time you ride.

What to look for in a bicycle helmet

We endorse these guidelines for bicycle helmets recommended by the American Academy of Pediatrics:

- The helmet should meet the voluntary testing standards of one of these two groups: American National Standards Institute (ANSI) or Snell Memorial Foundation. Look for a sticker on the inside of the helmet.

- Select the right size. Find one that fits comfortably and doesn't pinch.

- Buy a helmet with a durable outer shell and a polystyrene liner. Be sure it allows adequate ventilation.

- Use the adjustable foam pads to ensure a proper fit at the front, back and sides.

- Adjust the strap for a snug fit. The helmet should cover the top of your forehead and not rock side to side or back and forth with the chin strap in place.

- Replace your helmet if it is involved in an accident.

---

* Reprinted from July 1989 "Mayo Clinic Health Letter" with permission of Mayo Foundation, for Medical Education and Research, Rochester, Minnesota

The proper equipment for our intended level of biking is an important factor in your safety and enjoyment. All bike shops offer a wide selection of equipment, accessories and clothing and can best advise you on your specific needs.

Basic Equipment

1. The bicycle should fit your body size. The seat and handlebars should be adjusted to give you the maximum comfort for an extended trip. Your bike shop professional will help you with this.

2. Touring seats and handlebars are more comfortable for casual biking. Racing handlebars put considerable pressure on wrists and hands in addition to the strain on your neck from riding with your hands so low. Touring seats are wider and generally carry more padding -- something most people appreciate. You can buy seat pads filled with gel or made of soft and comfortable sheepskin.

3. The angle of the seat is critical. It should be level and the height set so the leg is nearly fully extended when the pedal is in the full down position.

Accessories

Realizing there are a multitude of accessories available, we will confine our comments to a very few which we have found to be most beneficial to our biking safety and pleasure. The most important, the helmet, is discussed at length on page 102.

1. Seat pads filled with gel provide multiple return on the investment in the form of added comfort.

2. Padded bike shorts reduce chafing, absorb moisture and provide additional padding.

3. Helmet rear view mirror is primarily a safety accessory but it also saves neck strain.

4. Padded gloves help reduce discomfort of weight and tension on the hands when subject to long periods in the same position.

5. Frame mounted water bottle should be translucent to keep track of supply.

Special Equipment

It is not necessary for certain equipment to be carried by everyone, but it is desirable that someone in the group carry a tire pump, patching material and some basic tools.

For example:
>Screwdriver
>6" or 8" adjustable wrench
>Pair of small pliers
>Accurate tire pressure gauge

Everyone should carry at least one bike bag. How many, size and style depend on the type of ride and length of trip you intend to make.

We recommend a handle bar bag for clothing and personal items on every bike. One insulated rear wheel bag is adequate for every two people. This may require a rear carrier bracket. Use one or two reusable containers of frozen liquid to ensure cold drinks and preserve food.

If your bike trip is an overnight, you will require larger saddle bag storage for extra clothing. Saddle bags are available for either front or back wheels.

Transportation

There are a multitude of ways to transport your bicycle. Those who own a van, enclosed truck or motorhome, have a convenient as well as secure method. Roof top and rear trunk or bumper racks are perhaps the most common with only the more expensive providing theft security.

When a group is traveling some distance to a biking destination, the number of vehicles becomes a factor. It may be desirable for each vehicle to transport four or more bikes, or to have a unit which will transport a number of bikes.

Our group accomplishes this by having a mid-size open pickup and an open trailer available. Each will hold four bikes using built-in racks and rubber tie downs. The trailer also works well with any auto with a trailer hitch. This does not provide the best security so it may be necessary to take your bike indoors with you if staying overnight.

Bike Shorts

• A large plastic garbage bag takes little space and makes good emergency rain cover.

• A perfect ride begins with the right safety gear and supplies.